JOB'S WIFE

A Play

(Inspired by the biblical story of Job)

PHILIP BEGHO

Monarch Books

JOB'S WIFE

First Published 2002

Email: monarch_books@yahoo.com
Tel: +234 8060069597

ISBN 978-32224-5-7

PUBLISHED BY MONARCH BOOKS
NIGERIA

JOB'S WIFE

JOB'S WIFE

C H A R A C T E R S

JOB'S WIFE.

REIBAH, A middle-aged woman.   ) Maids to
) Job's
NALI, A teen-aged girl.   ) wife.

THE HEALER, A young man of some mystery.

SCENE: The entire action takes place in the
       sleeping chamber of Job's wife. About
       537 BC.

Job's Wife

JOB'S WIFE'S sleeping chamber – a large room strewn with clothing and packing trunks.

JOB'S WIFE and REIBAH are packing in mournful silence. JOB'S WIFE stops for a while to observe REIBAH.

JOB'S WIFE:

Reibah!

REIBAH:

Madam?

JOB'S WIFE:

Your hands dawdle, then shuffle awry!

REIBAH:

Madam?

JOB'S WIFE:

You are making linen of silk! Behold, here –
Silk in a trunk for linen! Oh, Reibah!
What has seized you and left you with Nali's
   mind?

REIBAH:

Oh madam…

JOB'S WIFE:

Though time-pressed I would not have Nali
   do this –
Her hands think with the flutter of a child
And make an endless grief of endeavor;
But you? And when I most need diligence?

REIBAH:

Madam, your leaving addles me useless.

JOB'S WIFE:

We must be strong, Reibah; strong and
    stalwart! –
Greeting occasion with bronze temper,
And with stern mettle all life's maladies.

REIBAH:

But if you leave, madam, what will become
    of us?

JOB'S WIFE:

You will sink, and then you will rise as you
    must.

REIBAH:

My lady, I pray you, stay!

JOB'S WIFE:

If I stayed, would it do good, make rust
   gold,
Give blood and breath and bread to powdery
   bones
And make your wages outlive Job's
   fortunes,
Which daily shrink in night's lethal grip?

REIBAH:

Show me who, madam, will not gladly forgo
At such a time as this, wages' limb and bulk
To keep alive the heart and pulse of her
   service?

JOB'S WIFE:

All the pulse is dead, Reibah, all the heart;
Nothing but a lying shadow remains.
Now to work! Quick! The time bears hard
   behind

And day departs; I must leave ere the
  groaning starts.

REIBAH:
Oh, madam…

JOB'S WIFE:
To work, Reibah; to work!
[*Silence, while they continue packing.*]

REIBAH:
Madam!

JOB'S WIFE:
What now?

REIBAH:
There is a man, a certain man, a healer…

JOB'S WIFE:

Leave off!

REIBAH:

This man…

JOB'S WIFE:

All the healers of Uz and regions known,
Heads aloft with the boast of herbs and
    powers,
Have beaten path to the portals of Job's
    abode
And shuffled back anon whence they came,
Their herbs unavailing, their powers
    shamed,
Their heads double bent in double sorrow.
No, Reibah, lift not the heart with lying
    hope.

REIBAH:

This man comes from afar…

JOB'S WIFE:

Too far for me! When he comes, I'll be
  gone!

REIBAH:

Madam, he's near…

JOB'S WIFE:

What nonsense, Reibah; he's far and he's
  near!
What nonsense foolishness makes your
  mouth eat!

REIBAH:

I meant, madam…

JOB'S WIFE:
Work, Reibah, work!

REIBAH:
I meant…
[*Knock on the door.*]

JOB'S WIFE:
Is that Nali?
[*Enter* NALI.]
Nali, is he dead?

NALI:
No, madam.

JOB'S WIFE:
Is he dying?

NALI:
He is talking.

JOB'S WIFE:

Talking?

NALI:

He bemoans his fate to the comforters:

His friends – Lords Eliphaz, Bildad and
Zophar.

JOB'S WIFE:

At last, the man speaks! He opens his
mouth!

Soon he will do it: he will curse God and
die!

REIBAH:

Madam, I meant – I meant – I meant,
madam…

JOB'S WIFE:

Reibah, what has seized you? What a flutter!

REIBAH:

I meant, madam, that he comes from a
    distant land,
But he's close by now, in the neighbor-
    hood.
I heard whispers at noon. He arrived today.

JOB'S WIFE:

Leave off. So he speaks, Nali, does he?

NALI:

He curses the day of his birth.

JOB'S WIFE:

Let him curse God and die!

NALI:

Oh, madam, do not speak thus.

REIBAH:

Madam, this healer…

JOB'S WIFE:

Reibah, Job needs no healer but repentance.

All know his affliction is most unnatural:

It is punishment from the hand of God.

He has sinned against God; we know, and he
    knows –

But his pride shuts off repentance, hardens
    him;

He will not bow or yield to confession,

Will not in sorrow acknowledge his guilt,

And for this reason he suffers hell on earth –

And would drag us into his willful torment.

But no more! He'll have me no more in his
    hell!

From the bonds that hold me captive in Job's
    hell

I loose myself and this very day walk free!

NALI:

Of what healer does Reibah speak?

REIBAH [*to* NALI]:

If madam leaves, what would become of us?

NALI:

Reibah, what healer is this?

JOB'S WIFE:

Pack, Reibah! Nali, attend! No, touch
   nothing!

Should I let your butterfly hands dance here

To make flitting sport and puzzle of order?

Well, Nali, if you'd be serious for once –

Attend the fine linen, the red and blue
   flimsies;

The red ones go here, and the blue there –
   yes.

NALI:

Has Reibah found a healer then?

JOB'S WIFE:

No more talk about healers; bend to work.

REIBAH:

But what harm could come of it, my lady?

JOB'S WIFE:

To work!

REIBAH:

Just let him try.

NALI:

If Reibah has found a healer…

JOB'S WIFE:

Pack, pack!

REIBAH:

He would be here in no time…

NALI:

Give him a try, madam.

JOB'S WIFE:

Not there, Nali! Any with a touch of red –
    here!

NALI:

As Reibah says, there can be no harm.

REIBAH:

Why would madam not consider it?

JOB'S WIFE:

Nali! Here!

NALI:

No harm at all!

REIBAH:

He may just be the one…

NALI:

Who can tell how healing may come?

REIBAH:

Just try him, madam; try him!

NALI:

There can be no harm at all!

REIBAH:

Why does madam hesitate? Time presses.

NALI:

Let it not be said that madam, in need,

Loitered by, contemptuous of endeavor.

Give not tongues free wag, though wag as
they might,

They would not out-speak madam's
conscience,

Which forever would peel lips to accuse:

'If perhaps I had done … Perhaps if I had
done…'

JOB'S WIFE:

Oh! Oh! Must I be assailed at every turn?

Must the points of the air all combine to
pierce me?

Must my ears be beaten with words to draw
blood?

What do you want of me, what seek to
extract?

Here! Take, Reibah! Go and find your
healer!

Go to your healer – and leave me to find my

peace!

No, wait! Give me back the money! Give
    me!

Must I pay for Job's folly with Job's wife's
    coin?

Let Job pay with his own purse, not his
    wife's!

Stay, Reibah, while I fetch what is his.

[Exit.

REIBAH:

What will I do, Nali? I'm caught in sinking
    sand:

I know not of any healer – I told a lie!

NALI:

What, Reibah! The healer was invented?

REIBAH:

I know not what threw me to it. No, it leapt

up,
Threw itself tongue-ward, and of its own
   accord
Came forth from my lips, tumbling with all
   its force
And invention, shaming any restraint,
Arresting all qualms, as truth often does:
Only this is no truth – it's a lie.

NALI:
Then tarry awhile till time reaps you truth.

REIBAH:
What?

NALI:
Give remorse to time as seed for sowing;
And time, that silent worker of marvels,
That quiet laborer whose field teems
   strange crops,

May harvest wonders and reap you truth.

REIBAH:

What curious thoughts gather in you, Nali;

Is this fitting time for butterfly twirls?

NALI:

Twirl or no, nothing may be done but to woo
time;

Go, Reibah, with remorse and trade with
time.

REIBAH:

Go where?

NALI:

Anywhere. Range round. Roam the fields.
Dawdle.

Who knows: a cure may come ere you return

To liberate and from your lie release you;

And while you are gone madam will tarry.

REIBAH:
You must not let her leave.

NALI:
She will wait.

REIBAH:
You will keep her?

NALI:
She will wait.

REIBAH:
Oh, what sweet relief salves my brow, my
    lids,
And on my thoughts and ire lays soothing
    balm!
Nali, how sweet sense and nonsense do at

once

Embrace you, enfold you, and around you

Ever raise the flutter or beating wings

Of silly butterfly or knowing owl!

You are young and yet old, old and but a
     child,

And leave me lost and ever bewildered.

I will do as you say, nor have any choice.

NALI:

If you must know, Reibah, it worries me

That I flirt with sense and dance with
     nonsense

Till I know not who is who. But hush! She
     comes…

[*Re-enter* JOB'S WIFE.]

JOB'S WIFE:

Here, Reibah! Give him this ring. Pure
     gold –

Useless to Job but not to men of sense.

Nali! Do you idle about? Work! Work!

REIBAH:

Will madam not delay her packing,

Stay it till I return with news this way or
that?

JOB'S WIFE:

Begone, Reibah! Leave me to my resolve!

REIBAH [*going*]:

Nali…

NALI:

But trust me.

[*Exit* REIBAH.

JOB'S WIFE:

Nali, bend to work! Bend to work!

[*They pack in silence a while.*]

NALI:

Madam?

JOB'S WIFE:

No nonsense from you now, Nali.

NALI:

This is full serious, madam.

JOB'S WIFE:

What is it?

NALI:

Must you go, madam?

JOB'S WIFE:

And that is full serious?

NALI:

Yes, madam.

[*Silence a while.*]

Madam?

[*Silence.*]

Madam?

[*Silence.*]

Madam?

[*Silence.*]

Madam, believe me, this is full, full serious.

JOB'S WIFE:

What now, Nali! What?

NALI:

Madam, must you *really, really* go?

JOB'S WIFE:

Oh, Nali! I shut my ears hence to all
   needling

And snatch my face from folly's wheedle!

[*Silence a while.*]

NALI [*song-like tone*]:

Take me along with you when you go,
    madam.

Please, madam, please. Take me along with
    you.

I won't be a burden to you, I promise.

I won't be any trouble, no trouble at all.

[*Ignored utterly by* JOB'S WIFE *who spares
not a glance her way,* NALI, *henceforth,
comically and ostentatiously proceeds, as
she sings below, to sabotage the packing,
e.g. she tries on dresses behind* JOB'S
WIFE'S *back, hangs things up rather than
fold them, and ceaselessly folds and unfolds
others.*]

[*singing*]

I'm no strain or trouble at all

Nor any pain to anyone:

I bow and bend and do my work

As pleasing as pleasing can be.

And I don't eat much, no I don't,

Except for breakfast, lunch and tea

Or the plate or two at supper –

And that's nothing compared to you.

And here and there and everywhere

We'll have our things packed up in sacks,

As happy as happy can be;

And when two beds may not be had,

No sweat, madam, we'll take just one,

And on the floor we'll lay you down

And right up the bed I'll snuggle.

Oh, what great fun we'll always have,

I'm not any trouble at all.

[JOB'S WIFE *finally catches* NALI *relaxing on her divan.*]

JOB'S WIFE:
Nali!

NALI [*not rising*]:
Yes, madam?

JOB'S WIFE:
Nali…

NALI:
Madam?

JOB'S WIFE:
What madness has out-Nalid you?

NALI:
If you won't take me with you…

JOB'S WIFE:
Up! Now! Up, I say! Up!

NALI:
I'm not any trouble at all.

JOB'S WIFE:

The door screams!

NALI: Screams?

JOB'S WIFE:

For you! Now out!

NALI [*singing*]:

If I were to go…

JOB'S WIFE: Out!

NALI [*singing*]:

Where, madam, I pray, would I go?

[*Reclines across doorway, sucking her thumb.*]

JOB'S WIFE:

Out! Out! Out, I say! Out!

[*Exit* NALI, *wiggling her fingers in a coy goodbye gesture.*

JOB'S WIFE:

Oh! Oh that I have lived to see such ruins,

Such a falling apart of my world!

Night when it is yet noon, darkness ere
    dusk!

My own maidservant, my own servant
    mocks me –

An urchin, a street orphan plucked by Job

From the slimy claim of gutterous death –

She mocks me, and all on account of Job!

Everything now mocks me because of Job:

The air, my life, the seasons, everything –

They mock me, shame me, strip me woeful
    bare,

Lift me naked aloft and hurl me down
    bereft!

O God, what is my sin? Where have I erred?

How offended? It was but yesterday,

A little time gone past, and the land of Uz,

Her maids and all her women-folk, envied
me –

Job's wife, the one who married honor
himself;

Job's wife, the favored one, who in
marriage

Received the hand of righteousness,
complete,

As man may have, and mortal mould
display.

Job's wife, perfect hew of Eastern women
blessed!

Riches and honor, children and love and
health –

All were mine; my life was whole and
rounded,

Fresh and gladsome as the air at dewy dawn,

And then the Sabeans came with thirsty

swords,
And lo! the fire hurtling from heaven,
And ere the news was heard the slaughtering
   Chaldeans!
And oh! – oh! – the wind across the desert
And in one day my fruit manifold gone!
Tortured day! Tortured day and season vile!
Left with one who is nor man nor husband –
A barely breathing piece of putrid flesh,
A crawling covert for maggots and flies!
What is my offense, how have I
   transgressed?
Once the toast of Eastern women, now the
   shame!
And all for Job! Job of Uz whom I wed –
And would not, had I but seen with prescient
   eye
The end and dishonor of tainted
   righteousness!
But no more! Today the bird escapes her

snare

And before the groaning starts, wings aloft!

[*She resumes her packing with new vigor.*]

[*Enter* THE HEALER.]

[*He 'appears' rather than 'enters'.* JOB'S WIFE *is so engrossed that it is a while before she senses a foreign presence.*]

JOB'S WIFE: [*turning slowly, apprehensively, and seeing him*]:

What? Who? Who are you? Oh … Oh … the
    healer…

What a fright … What a fright you gave! Oh
    me!

Who would have thought you'd make it here
    so soon –

And not this way. No, not this way at all.

And not so soon, too. So Reibah … Reibah
    found you…

You live near then? Oh, what a fright! You
    live near?

THE HEALER:

No.

JOB'S WIFE:

Far away?

THE HEALER:

Yes. But I'm always near.

JOB'S WIFE:

Had you but come a little later, well…

As you can see, boxes and trunks and
    cases…

I'll be gone soon. Oh, how you startled me!

The red things go in here, and the blue there.

There are other colors, too, but red and
    blue…

Did glories more gorgeous ever nick the
    eye?

Healer, have you favorite colors?

Oh me, what drivel dribbles down my chin!

THE HEALER:

And where is Job's wife bound?

JOB'S WIFE:

It was silly of her – Reibah, you know…

It was silly of her, letting you in –

A little herald from her, courtesy's priming
    word…

THE HEALER:

Where, Lady Job, are you bound?

JOB'S WIFE:

But courtesy has scorned to bend here lately;

A strange and curious anarchy visits –

Nali's antics but a beat or two ago:

Mutiny's masterpiece carved in mahogany
    true!

And you…

THE HEALER:
True, my question begs an answering.

JOB'S WIFE:
Men never come into my chamber –
And strangers? Never! Nor for flame nor
    fire.
But may I call it my chamber still?
It's just borrowed now; I'm as good as gone.

THE HEALER:
Where to?

JOB'S WIFE:
Anywhere but where Job is.

THE HEALER:
Why?

JOB'S WIFE:

Why? How you question! Why! Did not
    Reibah say?

Can you not smell it? The air here is sick

With sin, guilt, offense! Ill deeds against
    God!

Defilement has pitched tent here, contagion
    reigns,

And I from sin's plague must detach myself!

THE HEALER:

Whose sin?

JOB'S WIFE:

Did Reibah bring you here with tongue roof-
    glued?

Have the region's prattlers so soon found
    other news

That the lips of Uz now desert Job's matter?

THE HEALER:

And what is his sin?

JOB'S WIFE:

To know you must find his heart and bid it
    speak;
My voice is rasping-hoarse from all asking;
Nor may his friends squeeze from him the
    utterance.

THE HEALER:

So none knows his sin.

JOB'S WIFE:

None.

THE HEALER:

But he has sinned?

JOB'S WIFE:

See for yourself; see the man and say.

See what was once living flesh and speak.

The flesh has died upon him and he lives
    still.

He has worms for flesh and boils for skin,

But breath yet issues from him, he would
    not die.

Flies wrap him as a shroud but he is no
    corpse.

Do you not smell the air, vile vapors
    abroad?

'Tis the stench from him, his flesh, his
    breath.

'Tis his sin: who but God may afflict man
    so?

Where but from God may such disaster
    come?

THE HEALER:

Satan, too, boasts such power.

JOB'S WIFE:

Satan can touch no man unless God allows.

And God will give no leave unless man has
   sinned.

It is the groaning – oh! – I most dread.

It comes at dusk and ceases not till dawn.

All evening, through the endless night, the
   groaning!

Nothing stifles it, nothing may quench it.

It overthrows slumber, slaughters sleep!

Oh dreadful dragon of night, tenor dread!

But no more! Tonight I shall find sleep,

For anywhere but here is slumber's heaven!

And you, will you not be gone to your task?

Me, I must hurry and be done with mine,

For I must escape ere the groaning starts.

THE HEALER:

You would escape your husband?

JOB'S WIFE:

Husband? No more. May dead flesh

husband a wife?

[*She listens, as one straining to hear a sound.*]

No! No! No! Not now! 'Tis not the hour!

It cannot be! No! 'Tis not the groaning!

I do not hear the groaning – I refuse!

'Tis not the hour! I do not hear it! Oh!

I must be gone! I must be gone! I must be

gone!

[*She resumes her packing in a frenzy, and tries from time to time to stifle the sound – inaudible to the audience – by clapping her hands to her ears, etc.*]

THE HEALER:

I will go to him.

JOB'S WIFE:

But go!

For what have you come but to go to him?

Go! Go!

  [*Exit* THE HEALER.

[*Alone, crying 'No!' 'No!' intermittently,*
JOB'S WIFE, *by various antics, tries with
rising desperation to mitigate the sound
until in hysterical climax she wraps a heap
of clothes round her head, then abandons
her efforts and breaks down sobbing. Then
she notices the groaning has ceased.*]

It has ceased! Has it ceased? It *has* ceased!

I hear nothing now! Or do I hear? No! No!

Nothing! It *has* ceased! It has! So soon! Oh!

Wonderful day! Wonderful, wonderful day!

Never before! Not ever! Not so soon! Oh…

[*Knock on the door. Enter* NALI.]

Nali! Nali, or do my ears deceive?

It has ceased, it has ceased, has it not?

NALI:

The groaning, madam? It has!

JOB'S WIFE:

So it has! So soon!

NALI:

To the world's surprise, madam! Most
welcome!

JOB'S WIFE:

He did it!

NALI:

Yes, madam.

JOB'S WIFE:

What great powers he must possess!

NALI:

Incomparable!

JOB'S WIFE:

Truly great!

NALI:

Beyond our imagination's span.

JOB'S WIFE:

You think so?

NALI:

Think so, madam? I *know* so!

JOB'S WIFE:

Nali, are you but certain?

NALI:

But of course! Does not the world know?

JOB'S WIFE:

Think – if he could make the groaning
  cease,

Cannot he also have him completely healed?

NALI:

But of course, madam, He can!

JOB'S WIFE:

Do you comprehend your purport, child?

NALI:

Think – does He begin a thing

But to have it annulled, disabled?

It must be that the master has confessed,

And He has in mercy forgiven him.

JOB'S WIFE:

What are you saying, child? Has your
  madness come?

Surely, you do not suggest he may forgive
   sins?

NALI:
But of course, madam! Who can if not He?

JOB'S WIFE:
Oh, Nali's madness has visited again,
And curves her tongue to wild and wicked
   blasphemy!

NALI:
Blasphemy?

JOB'S WIFE:
Oh Nali…

NALI:
Blasphemy, to say only God forgives sins?

JOB'S WIFE:

God?

NALI:

But, madam, who forgives sins but God?

JOB'S WIFE:

Nali, you dare suggest *that* man is God?

NALI:

What man?

[*Pause.*]

JOB'S WIFE [*laughing now*]:

Oh Nali! You silly little daft thing!

Did you think I spoke all the while of God?

No, Nali, I spoke of none but the man.

NALI:

What man, madam?

JOB'S WIFE:

The healer! You daft thing!

NALI:

The healer?

JOB'S WIFE:

Now go and have some wine sent up to me!

Large relief and hope less than relief

But handsome still, join to pique my palate

   for wine

Which the ravage of preceding days

Had robbed me of. Quickly, Nali, be off!

NALI:

Yes, madam.

      [*Exit.*

JOB'S WIFE:

Nali! Nali!

NALI [*re-entering*]:
Yes, madam?

JOB'S WIFE:
Why did you come?

NALI:
You called.

JOB'S WIFE:
No, Nali, not now.

NALI:
When?

JOB'S WIFE:
When you came after the groaning stopped.

NALI:
It is of that I speak, madam.

JOB'S WIFE:

I called you?

NALI:

Yes.

JOB'S WIFE:

After the groaning ceased?

NALI:

Yes.

JOB'S WIFE:

Me?

NALI:

Yes, madam.

JOB'S WIFE:

Not me.

NALI:

You, madam.

I heard you. Clear as tinkle-tinkle, winkle-
inkle.

JOB'S WIFE [*turning her back to her*]:

Just go, Nali.

Go before your madness erupts fiery.

Let the wine be dry, as befits the hour,

And let Reibah make me a meal, just above
light.

[THE HEALER '*appears' by the door.*]

NALI:

Reibah?

JOB'S WIFE:

Wine, dry; a meal a shade above light. Go.

NALI:

Yes, madam.

> [*Exit.*

JOB'S WIFE [*turning to the door and seeing* THE HEALER]:

Oh! You're there! I had no idea!

And Nali said nothing? Nali! Nali!

NALI [*re-entering*]:

Madam?

JOB'S WIFE: [*to* THE HEALER]:

She was toddling off for wine.

[*To* NALI] Two goblets, and wine enough.

NALI:

Madam?

THE HEALER:

Thank you, but my palate shuns the stuff.

JOB'S WIFE:

Nothing to refresh you?

NALI:

Pardon, madam?

THE HEALER:

Nothing.

JOB'S WIFE:

But a meal, surely.

[*To* NALI]

Have Reibah prepare a nice meal for him.

NALI:

Pardon, madam?

THE HEALER:

No, no. My palate speaks otherwise.

JOB'S WIFE:

Not even a broth?

NALI:

Me, madam?

THE HEALER:

No; but thanks.

NALI:

Me?

JOB'S WIFE:

Oh Nali, must you forever act the clown?

[*To* THE HEALER]

Whatever will I do with her!

[*To* NALI] Go!

THE HEALER:

More my fault, if truth be told, than hers.

JOB'S WIFE:

Not her fault? Well, maybe not. No one here

Has quite managed to remain happily sane:

Job's afflictions … Nali! You tarry! And

    stare! Go!

NALI:

Is madam well?

JOB'S WIFE:

Is madam well? Wobble Head calls up

    steam!

Be off now! Go! Go!

          [*Exit* NALI.

[*To* THE HEALER]

You stopped the groaning…

Can amazement outshine my wonder?

THE HEALER [*sitting down*]:

A little quiet does no harm –

Save when it bends the ear to men's mouths

In a season when ears should shrink from
words.

What friends they are – to make a man sin!

JOB'S WIFE:

Was it they who made him sin?

THE HEALER:

They have opened his mouth, prised loose
his tongue.

When mouths open before bitter adversity

Sin peeps out poised to lift the tongue to
offense.

Oh, what foolishness they have brought to
Job!

JOB'S WIFE:

Do you see them clothed in foolishness,

Those three robed wise in men's esteem?

THE HEALER:

Theirs is but the wisdom of erudition,

Bereft of discernment superior by far.

It is the foolish wise who embrace alone

Erudition and forsake wise discernment

Which clears the clouds and reveals the
    seasons:

The season for debate and for restraint,

For rebuke and for repair, to chide and
    cheer.

Job needed balming waters from the
    fountains

And springs of cool comfort and
    consolation,

But from his friends got only smothering tar

From the wells of argument and clamor.

JOB'S WIFE:

Should a man's friends not tell him when he
errs;

Not set his feet aright when he goes
transverse?

THE HEALER:

I see error sitting on other haunches,

Not on Job's, and walking transverse
elsewhere.

JOB'S WIFE:

Where?

THE HEALER:

Here.

JOB'S WIFE:

Here?

THE HEALER:

You were going to leave.

JOB'S WIFE:

And still will, if the season brings no rain.

THE HEALER:

Spousal desertion – is that not error

Of magnitude wicked, contemptible…

JOB'S WIFE:

How dare you!

THE HEALER:

…Despicable and damned, when the hour

Most begs your love, affection and duty!

JOB'S WIFE:

You insult me?

THE HEALER [*as though straining to hear something*]:

Shh!

JOB'S WIFE:

Insult me to my face?

THE HEALER:

He groans again!

JOB'S WIFE [*straining for the sound*]:

I hear nothing…

THE HEALER:

I must attend.

      [*Exit*.

JOB'S WIFE:

I hear nothing!

[*Knock on the door. Enter* NALI *with wine.*]

Nali! Do you hear anything! Listen…

Do you hear anything – the groaning?

NALI [*listening*]:

No; there is nothing.

JOB'S WIFE:

But he said the groaning had begun again.

NALI:

Who?

JOB'S WIFE:

Listen! I hear it!

NALI:

Indeed, madam, I can hear it now.

JOB'S WIFE:

It began only now, not so, Nali?

NALI:

Yes, madam.

JOB'S WIFE:

But he heard it before it began!

NALI:

Who, madam?

JOB'S WIFE:

Oh Nali! What must I make of this!

Give me some wine! Mind-numbing nectar!

NALI [*pouring her wine*]:

Madam is unwell.

JOB'S WIFE [*clapping her hands to her ears*]:

Oh! Oh! Oh!

NALI:

Madam would do well

To postpone her departure till she is well.

JOB'S WIFE [*dropping her hands from her ears*]:

But I must be brave; it may well cease again.

But if it lingers, I'll just eat and leave:

What I haven't packed, I haven't packed!

Oh, this sound, how it scrapes my spine!

What mind-numbing edible is Reibah

finding me?

NALI:

Reibah?

JOB'S WIFE:

Don't play the fool, girl!

Hurry Reibah up! I must eat and be gone!

[NALI *backs away, watching* JOB'S WIFE *with a puzzled expression*.]

[*Seeing her puzzled expression*]

Nali!

NALI:

Madam?

JOB'S WIFE [*suspiciously*]:

Reibah is busy at the stove, true or not?

NALI:

Well…

JOB'S WIFE:

Well what! You told her – you told her,
    Nali?

NALI:

I could not, madam. She wasn't there.

But in the kitchen the cooks are busy –

JOB'S WIFE:

I need no faceless busy cooks –

Reibah is Reibah! You know that!

She *only* satisfies me now that rebellion

In the house of Job has displayed ensign!

She wasn't there? Where then – where is
   she?

NALI:

Does madam forget?

She sent Reibah to fetch a healer.

JOB'S WIFE:

Nali, must you forever remain a child?

[*Singing*]

Little girl, little girl, Reibah is back,

She's been back, little girl, oh for a while;
Little girl, little girl, now go down to her
And have her, little girl, bring me a meal.
[*Speaking*]
Listen! Do you hear aught? The groaning –
The groaning has stopped; I daresay it has!

NALI:
It has, madam, and for a while –
[*Singing*]
While you were little-ing me all over town.

JOB'S WIFE:
He's done it again! How so wonderful!
Praise be to God who found Reibah the
  man!
If he can make it stop for good, I promise
I'll forgive him the bulk of his slanders.
Praise be to God!
[*Singing*]

Now go, little girl, and bounce Reibah here.

[*Exit* NALI, *puzzled.*

[JOB'S WIFE *continues her packing. Enter* THE HEALER.]

JOB'S WIFE [*suddenly noticing him*]:

Oh – you! What a fright again! I must ask,

Must insist on a knock and some herald,

Can't have you appearing – well – angel-

    like…

[*She laughs nervously at this.*]

Never mind how you made the groaning

    stop,

If you could but make it stop for good…

THE HEALER:

That would depend on you.

JOB'S WIFE:

Me?

THE HEALER:

Yes. You and the friends of Job, the people –

All the witnesses of Job's misfortune.

JOB'S WIFE:

What have we to do with it?

THE HEALER:

More than you'd want. You are to learn.

Are you learning? How quickly then? How
    well?

JOB'S WIFE:

I comprehend not.

THE HEALER:

Ever alive in the corpse of calamity

Is instruction. But instruction for whom?

The smitten? Not always, or not only.

The witnesses, sometimes, are in the main

Intended to be the event's beneficiaries.

They must observe, question, interpret,

Examine their hearts, and this is prime –

Unwrap their covering garments of deceit,

See their soul in all its nakedness,

Admit its truth, learn and be instructed.

The smitten, sometimes, is merely he found
   worthy

To bear the suffering that instructs his
   fellows;

And for this service his reward is sure,

Unalterable, for God is a just God,

Abiding no indebtedness to man.

Now from this calamity, Job's affliction,

What instruction has Job's wife found?

She has learnt, I think, spousal desertion –

Skill of departure at unwanted time.

In fair weather she says, 'Let none grudge
   me

That I of Job's prosperity do partake:

He is my husband, his portion is mine.'
But in tempest she says, 'I must detach
    myself;
No flesh is no husband, my portion lies
    abroad.'
Job's wife is nothing but a common harlot,
The most ignoble run of fortune-seekers
Who may, with the fair-weather coin of
    fortune,
Be bought and sold and market-haggled.

JOB'S WIFE:
No!

THE HEALER:
No?

JOB'S WIFE:
I have turned away because his sin is great,
And I must do my duty to God

And from great sin against God separate
    myself.

THE HEALER:

Oh? Had his fortunes, despite his sin,
    remained,
Would you nonetheless have deserted him
In order to do your duty to God?

JOB'S WIFE:

Yes!

THE HEALER:

So it is not the stench of his condition,
His ulcerous fortunes, that drive you off?

JOB'S WIFE:

By no means!

THE HEALER:

It is his sin alone?

JOB'S WIFE:

Yes!

THE HEALER:

If he confessed his sin and was forgiven,

You would stay and once more be wife to
  him?

JOB'S WIFE:

Yes!

THE HEALER:

Even if his stench and ulcers remained,

And his groaning continued to slay your
  nights?

[*Pause.*]

JOB'S WIFE:

If he confessed his sin and was forgiven,
The evidence of sin would not remain.

THE HEALER:

But if it did?

JOB'S WIFE:

It would not!

THE HEALER:

If you speak true, and it is but duty to God,
Not things mercenary lending you legs,
You would stay if no sin was found in Job.

JOB'S WIFE:

Yes!

THE HEALER:

Even if his stench and ulcers lingered.

JOB'S WIFE:

Yes!

THE HEALER:

For it is not his stench or ulcers,

Or groaning or other ills that drive you off.

JOB'S WIFE:

Yes! Yes! Yes! But who are you to treat me
thus?

What right have you to assail, knuckle me
down?

THE HEALER:

Listen!

JOB'S WIFE:

I have listened forever!

THE HEALER:

Can you not hear? He groans again.

JOB'S WIFE:

Yes, I hear it; and if you'd but go to him

And use time as you ought, milking from
  Job

Fitting confession rather than pummeling
  me,

You might cap the dragon's udder dry!

THE HEALER:

I go, but ponder still your ways.

[*Exit.*

[*Knock on the door. Enter* NALI, *with a tray of food.*]

JOB'S WIFE:

You Nali! Where is faithful Reibah?

NALI:

Faithful to your taste, I'm sure, is this meal,
  madam.

JOB'S WIFE:

Where is she!

NALI:

Not man nor mortal knowledge knows
  where Reibah,
Faithful to your healer-finding errand, lurks.

JOB'S WIFE:

None saw her bring him?

NALI:

None!

JOB'S WIFE:

Did the healer come on his own then?

NALI:

What healer, madam?

JOB'S WIFE:

Oh girl, how long must the fool's face mask
 you?

The healer – who's been attending Job!

NALI:

God only has been attending Lord Job.

JOB'S WIFE:

What depths of silly madness Nali
 measures!

Who stopped the groaning twice, I ask?

And now, do you hear aught? It has stopped
 but now.

Who, I ask, made this be? Who?

NALI:

No one but God, or Lord Job himself.

Happening by at its early start today,

I heard its fullness and heard its end.

It ceased – of its own accord, none
    commanding,

As it did second time coming, so the
    servants say.

Madam may send for them and bid them
    speak.

Or better, madam, better – go down,

Go yourself – and have the master himself
    speak.

JOB'S WIFE:

Nonsense!

NALI:

Pray, madam, why so?

JOB'S WIFE:

Mental wobble grows strong in you again.

NALI:

The stench sickens all and will sicken you,

But it slays none, nor will slaughter you.

JOB'S WIFE:

Begone from me!

NALI:

Why? So sweet an air chambers here.

JOB'S WIFE:

Begone!

NALI:

I'm never any trouble at all.

JOB'S WIFE:

Out! Out! Out I say!

        [*Exit* NALI.

Her madness by the hour grows and swells,

Bubbling and frothing to the very brim;

And I'm powerless to wrest her sane,

For sanity grows even alien to me

As questions query questions within,

Stirring this brain to hot and rabid delirium.

Oh that I'm not more caught in madness

Not to see this dispowering of my mind!

[*A loud and flamboyant knock on the door.
She is startled and remains still. The
knocking continues with increasing loudness
and flourish.*]

[*Going to the door*] What! What! What!

Why has madness brought anarchy to birth?

Why does chaos spring its furies but here!

[*Opening the door and seeing* THE
HEALER.] You!

THE HEALER [*entering*]:
Knock, said the lady.

JOB'S WIFE:
The world boils in lunacy's stew!

THE HEALER:
Rejoice; it is finished!

JOB'S WIFE [*pause*]:
Has the groaning died hopeless of life anew?

THE HEALER:
It has died for good, yes.

JOB'S WIFE:
Praise be to God! Praise be to the Most
High!
But… but how can we tell, be sure?

THE HEALER:

It has died for good.

JOB'S WIFE [*pause*]:

Is there … Is there hope he may be healed?

THE HEALER:

He *shall* be healed; he has confessed his sin.

JOB'S WIFE:

Can such brazen wonder find Job's house?

THE HEALER:

You hanker not to know his sin?

JOB'S WIFE:

Well?

THE HEALER:

He sinned when his mouth was prised open.

JOB'S WIFE:

When his friends came?

THE HEALER:

Yes.

JOB'S WIFE:

But his friends came because he was
    afflicted.

THE HEALER:

Yes.

JOB'S WIFE:

Because of his sin.

THE HEALER:

No, not because of his sin. Job was
    righteous,
More righteous by far than you or his

friends;
In all the earth there was none so righteous
And so blameless before God as the man
  Job.
He was afflicted, not for iniquity,
But to test him and all those around him.
He fell to offense only when his friends
  came
And scrabbled his soul to unleash bitterness.
For then in acrimony Job suggested
That God was unjust to afflict the righteous.
He offended there, for God is never unjust.
It is the privilege of the Lord God,
Our maker, the creator of all that is,
He who set the outposts of wisdom and
  knowledge,
The pillars of the rules that govern man,
In His wisdom to afflict a righteous man
In order to test him, to strengthen him,
To purify him, or to heroify him

For His glory's sake, or so that his fellows
May by his suffering be tested and schooled.
Job's friends have been schooled and now
    clearly see
That even the righteous may suffer
    affliction.
They have learnt new lessons of
    compassion;
But you, I ask you once again, what have
    you learnt?

JOB'S WIFE [*in rising apprehension*]:
What stench now floods the room in rising
    tide?
What smell assails, crashes upon us tempest-
    tossed?

THE HEALER:
It is the smell of Job.

JOB'S WIFE:

Job!

THE HEALER:

They are bringing Job here.

JOB'S WIFE:

Here!

THE HEALER:

They are bringing your husband to you.

JOB'S WIFE:

No! No! No! Not here! They mustn't bring
him here!

[*She flies into a panic and hysterically tries
to barricade the door.* THE HEALER *is
seated the while, watching her calmly.*]

I will not have him here! I cannot have him
here!

THE HEALER:

He is your husband.

JOB'S WIFE:

I cannot have him here – I cannot! No! No!

THE HEALER:

He crawls the road to recovery…

JOB'S WIFE:

Not in here! Not in here! No!

THE HEALER:

The stench diminishes with his healing.

JOB'S WIFE:

He must not come in here! No! No!

THE HEALER:

You turned your back to your husband, you

said,
Because of his sin, not the stench he
  became.

JOB'S WIFE:
Keep him away! Keep him away!

THE HEALER:
His sin is forgiven, he's without blame now.

JOB'S WIFE:
Not here! Not here! No! Keep him away!

THE HEALER:
Or were you escaping, deserting him
Because of his misfortune, his affliction?

JOB'S WIFE:
I'll not have him here! No! No! I'll not! I'll
  not!

[*She collapses in deep sobbing.* THE HEALER *goes to her.*]

THE HEALER:

Job's wife, search your heart, drive this lie

from you!

Why did you turn your back to your

husband?

Was it because of an imagined sin

Or was it because of a change of fortune?

[*Pause.* JOB'S WIFE *just keeps on sobbing.*]

Job's wife, answer! Why did you desert Job,

Turn your back to him, close your face, your

heart?

Why did you abandon your husband?

Was it because of an unproven sin

Or because of smell and sores and faltering

wealth?

JOB'S WIFE [*amidst tears*]:

I'm a woman: just flesh and blood and
    human heart;

There's only so much a woman can take,

Only so much the human heart will hold!

THE HEALER:

So you lied to yourself and to the world.

JOB'S WIFE:

What could I do?

THE HEALER:

You lied!

JOB'S WIFE:

Yes!

THE HEALER:

You lied! You lied!

JOB'S WIFE:

Yes! Yes!

THE HEALER:

And sinned against your husband and your
    God.

JOB'S WIFE:

Oh God! Oh my God, forgive me! Forgive
    me!

[*Pause.*]

THE HEALER:

Behold now, the smell is gone.

JOB'S WIFE:

Oh God…

THE HEALER:

They've borne him away.

JOB'S WIFE:

I sinned … I sinned…

THE HEALER:

Dry your tears now.

JOB' S WIFE:

I sinned…

THE HEALER:

With repentance comes forgiveness; dry
  your tears.

But you must go to your husband and make
  amends.

As for me, my work is done and I must be
  gone.

[*Exit.*

JOB'S WIFE *dries her tears and sits down,
puzzled and meditative.*]

[*A knock on the door. Enter* REIBAH,

shuffling forward tearfully.]

JOB'S WIFE:
Reibah!

REIBAH [*tearful*]:
My lady, will sorry be word enough?

JOB'S WIFE:
Reibah, what assails you?

REIBAH:
Sorry, my lady, sorry.

JOB'S WIFE:
Reibah…

REIBAH:
I lied. Will madam forgive me?

JOB'S WIFE:

You lied?

REIBAH:

I know not how it came, most uncommon…

JOB'S WIFE:

What did your tongue find, Reibah?

REIBAH:

The healer … Madam there is no healer – I
    lied!

What seized me defies knowing, what
    curved my tongue –

Perhaps to keep you from leaving – so
    desperate was I!

Oh madam … Will my lady forgive?

JOB'S WIFE:

What now is Reibah saying?

REIBAH:

Loitering by the stream, killing time,

I could hold the lie no longer…

JOB'S WIFE:

The healer was here, Reibah!

REIBAH:

I lied, madam, I lied; there's no healer!

[*Enter* NALI.]

NALI:

Reibah! It was indeed you then!

They caught a glimpse, they said, of Reibah,

Or perhaps her angel, sauntering

   chamber-ward.

JOB'S WIFE:

Nali! Tell me the truth, swear to me –

Did you or did you not see the healer?

NALI:

Oh madam! Why will madam not believe –

I know of no healer that visited

Nor of any stranger so resembling!

JOB'S WIFE:

That man…

NALI:

What man?

JOB'S WIFE:

He who was here…

NALI:

Here? Madam, here? A man? A stranger?

Madam will sooner have behemoth here!

JOB'S WIFE:

I let him in, Nali, though I know not why.

He was here, and you saw him, Nali; speak
    true.
I sent you for wine, and then called you back
    in,
Bidding you bring refreshments for him;
But he declined, demurring to eat or drink.

NALI:
I remember well, madam; it stuck –
You offered me, to my surprise – and
    delight –
You offered me wine, a meal, refreshment…

JOB'S WIFE:
Not you, the man.

NALI:
There was no man; we were alone, you and
    I.
But you did seem to be talking, I thought,

To someone else, not me. It worried me.

I thought you were … I thought you had,

    well…

I thought perhaps your cares had tilted the

    chamber up –

Though nothing, of course, a little rest could

    not repair…

[*Noises and shouts offstage.*]

JOB'S WIFE:

Clamor drives madness berserk!

NALI:

Should I venture forth to see, madam?

JOB'S WIFE:

Yes, yes!

     [*Exit* NALI.

[*To* REIBAH] There was a man … a man…

REIBAH:

A visitor, perhaps, of Lord Job's?

JOB'S WIFE:

No … No … He was a strange man – ah,
  yes…
No ordinary man … For no ordinary man
Could bring me crashing to my knees…
  Reibah!
[*She falls to her knees.*]

REIBAH:

Madam…!

JOB'S WIFE:

It was … an angel!

REIBAH:

Madam?

JOB'S WIFE:

God sent me an angel!

NALI [*offstage, running to them*]:

Madam! Madam! Madam!

[*Entering*]

Madam, the master! Lord Job! Lord Job…

JOB'S WIFE:

Has been healed.

NALI:

Madam!

REIBAH:

Healed?

JOB'S WIFE:

The angel said so, said his work was done.

REIBAH:

Can it be? Can it … be?

NALI:

His flesh is all healed – new and baby-like!
No smell! He stands and walks with strong
   gait!

REIBAH:

No!

JOB'S WIFE:

Yes! For God has visited the house of Job
With wings rich-plumed with mercy!

NALI:

Oh…!

JOB'S WIFE:

Praise be to the Living God, the Most High!

A God of compassion and abundant mercy,
Whose love overflows and endures forever,
And for whom nothing is too difficult!

REIBAH & NALI:
Glory be to God – in the highest!

Lights fail.

The End

About the Author

PHILIP BEGHO is the author of several award-winning books. His wide-ranging interest has seen him in a varied career that has spanned journalism, banking, business, legal practice and university teaching. He has also engaged in film and theatrical production.

He now works as a full-time writer, concentrating largely on children's literature and verse drama.

Job's Wife won the 2002 ANA/NDDC Drama Prize.

Verse plays by Philip Begho

www.ingramcontent.com/pod-product-compliance
Lightning Source LLC
Chambersburg PA
CBHW070018110426
42741CB00034B/2110